I0799315

LIFE IN THE MIDDLE AGES™

FASHION AND CLOTHING

MARGAUX BAUM AND
MARGARET SCOTT

rosen publishing's
rosen central®

NEW YORK

Published in 2017 by The Rosen Publishing Group
29 East 21st Street, New York, NY 10010

Copyright © 2017 by The Rosen Publishing Group, Inc.

First Edition

All rights reserved. No part of this book may be reproduced in any form without permission in writing from the publisher, except by a reviewer.

Library of Congress Cataloging-in-Publication Data

Names: Baum, Margaux, author. | Scott, Margaret, 1951– author.
Title: Fashion and clothing / Margaux Baum and Margaret Scott.
Description: First Edition. | New York : Rosen Publishing, 2017. | Series: (Life in the Middle Ages) | Includes bibliographical references, webography and index. | Audience: Grades: 5–8.
Identifiers: LCCN 2016030494 | ISBN 9781499464689 (Library Bound)
Subjects: LCSH: Clothing and dress—Europe—History—Medieval, 500-1500—Juvenile literature.
Classification: LCC GT575 .B38 2017 | DDC 391.009409/02—dc23
LC record available at https://lccn.loc.gov/2016030494

Manufactured in China

CONTENTS

INTRODUCTION

The Middle Ages in Europe were a time that still inspires great interest and sparks the imagination to this day. From about 500 CE and 1500 CE (the years generally accepted as the medieval era) science, religion, art, architecture, literature, and people's daily lifestyles and cultures were vastly different from our own.

Clothing is one of the more visible and distinctive aspects of medieval life that stands out in most people's mind. When it comes to wardrobe, our image of the Middle Ages has been formed from the countless paintings, murals, sculptures, manuscripts and other sources that document the era, as well as the countless films and television shows that depicted medieval life and events. Of course, there was a huge spectrum of clothing fashions and types that existed throughout medieval Europe. This changed dramatically, too, in the thousand years or so of the age.

Clothing was a very important part of the lives of medieval people, beyond simply the functional aspect of staying clothed. Much like today, people were judged by their appearance, including the clothing they wore, which was an indication of their social status.

Many medieval people, especially those with some means, or money, were pulled in different directions: On one hand, wealthy people were able to think about what they wore because clothes were expensive and they had the resources. At the same time, the Church tended to frown upon its members following fashion too desperately, or

The fashions of the middle ages may seem excessive and even outlandish to modern observers. This print shows the lavishly dressed Empress Matilda, a twelfth century claimant to the English throne.

being lavishly dressed. After all, vanity (or pride) is one of Catholicism's seven deadly sins.

Many medieval governments made laws that prevented or discouraged people of lower social status from wearing clothes that were too expensive or lavish, in part so that they were distinguishable from the noble classes. Such restrictions tended to be more relaxed, or even nonexistent, for the wealthy and powerful, especially the nobility.

From peasants and their functional, basic clothing, to rich merchants in their finery, to knights mobilizing for war, to kings and queens holding court at ceremonies and banquets, to clergy and members of monastic orders, clothing denoted one's station and profession very publicly. The availability of fabrics over time, changing morals, religion, exposure to the peoples of other nations, and interchange with both Europeans and non-Europeans—all these factors had a dramatic impact on medieval fashions and clothing.

CHAPTER ONE

CLOTHING IN MEDIEVAL LIFE

There are many variations of the saying, "the clothes make the person." This remains true, even as many people believe that what is within one's heart and mind that should matter more. For medieval people, appearances were as important as they are in modern life. This was especially true because medieval European people typically had more rigid, official social divisions than many modern Western cultures do. Whereas nowadays a person of modest means can wear a very similar outfit to that of a very wealthy one, during the middle ages this was far less likely, and often impossible. Dressing at a higher social station was very expensive and often illegal. For the most part, it was thus far easier to tell a peasant from an artisan or from a landed member of the gentry or nobility.

After the production of food, the most important medieval activity was the production of textiles, mostly for clothing. Fortunes were made from textiles, and therefore from clothing. Many cities in the Low Countries—the region now consisting of Belgium, Luxembourg, and the Netherlands—owed their wealth to the excellent woolen cloths that they wove and exported. In the 1360s, England began to export wool cloth, in addition to raw wool. Through this trade England became a wealthy country. Even today, in the House of Lords in London, the lord chancellor sits on a seat called the Woolsack, a symbol of the origins of England's wealth.

This fourteenth century manuscript from Italy depicts a merchant showing a customer a hide he is offering for sale. The Mediterranean region especially was an important epicenter of the textile trade.

In Italy, the local wool was of a fairly poor quality, and good woolen cloth was imported from northern Europe. In the city of Florence, the guilds of merchants who imported and finished such cloth grew very wealthy and powerful. Any man who wanted to be involved in the government of Florence had to belong to one of twenty-one guilds. He would have even more influence if he belonged to one of the seven "greater guilds." Of these seven greater guilds, three were textile guilds—the cloth finishers, the woolen cloth merchants, and the silk merchants. A fourth guild, that of the furriers, was also related to clothing production. The tailors in Florence, however, had no guild of their own until the sixteenth century. This was because their labor was cheap and materials were expensive. Customers took cloth they had purchased to a tailor and asked him to make clothes for them. This meant that tailors generally didn't own the materials they worked with, unlike the members of the greater guilds.

The most expensive woolen cloths were scarlets. We now think of scarlet as red. In the Middles Ages, however, the term scarlet referred to a very high quality cloth that was created through specific processes. Such cloth was often dyed a shade of red, from rose-pink to blood-red, using the most expensive dye called kermes. But scarlet cloth could also be green, blue, or even white. Laws often said that to wear scarlet you had to be at least a doctor or a knight. Kermes was also used to dye silks crimson. Silks could easily be much more expensive than scarlets, and crimson velvet cloth with gold trimming was probably the most expensive fabric made in Europe. Very few people wore it. Around 1100, Italian merchants imported kermes and silks from the Middle East and southern Spain, but Italy soon began making its own silks and exporting them far and wide.

Attending church for the first time after giving birth was an important event in a woman's life, and those who could afford to do so ordered new clothes for the occasion. For her "churching" in 1330, the queen of England had an outfit of five garments made of purple

This illustration depicts drapers at work. Drapers had an important trade guild during the middle ages, and mainly sold cloth and other fabrics.

velvet and embroidered with gold squirrels. Purple had been a royal color since Roman times.

CLASS, COUNTRY, AND CLOTHING

Fashionable clothing was available to very few people in the Middle Ages because of the cost and laws limiting access to fashionable materials and styles. And ideas could travel only as fast as people could.

Today, in a few hours we can make journeys that used to take people days or even months. Men traveled more than women, and men's dress was therefore quite similar in countries that were close to each other. Because women traveled so little, they tended to wear clothing that was fashionable mainly within their own cities. Local clothing styles were seen as a part of someone's nationality.

MEDIEVAL FASHION: A VISUAL RECORD

We all grow up with ideas about how people looked in the Middle Ages. Knights wore shining armor, and ladies wore tall, steeple-like hats with long veils floating from them. But where do we get these ideas? We rarely get the chance to see what actual medieval dress looked like because so little of it has survived. We have that picture of knights and ladies because of the sources on which we rely.

A THEORY OF FASHION

More and more people tried to wear fashionable clothing as the Middle Ages went on. One theory says that fashion begins when someone designs clothes that are not practical, and people become convinced that by wearing such clothes they can tell the world that they are special and up-to-date, leaders of taste and style.

At the same time, being fashionable means looking like everyone else who is fashionable, so you're not so special after all! Then the fashion leaders move on to wearing something else, because they don't want to look like everyone else who has just caught up with them. Then another fashion develops, and so on.

The Church and the authorities, worried by this seemingly endless thirst for novelty and the self-absorption that fashion created in its "victims," fought endlessly and with little success to persuade people to abandon fashion. Many efforts by religious and political authorities to curb fashion obsessions have also been loosely tied to morality. The medieval Church, in particular, warned against vanity as a moral failing.

Since about 1100, we have been seeking new ways to make our clothing more interesting and more attractive. Fashion has always annoyed some people, usually the older generation, who forget that they themselves once

annoyed their parents by the things they insisted on wearing! This book looks at ways in which people sought to look fashionable in the period from 1100 to 1500. These years were marked by an increasingly sophisticated ability to cut fabric to fit the body. As a result, among the fashionable, a slender body became the ideal.

The sources rarely indicate how crumpled clothes could look, or how dirty the roads could make them, or how little they and their wearers were washed.

To find out about medieval clothes, one of the most important sources we have are the illuminated manuscripts produced for use by the clergy or by rich laymen and laywomen. Sometimes we know when manuscripts were produced, and sometimes we can work it out. By the end of the fifteenth century, many wealthy people commissioned illuminated prayer books called Books of Hours. The affluent owners of these Books of Hours often appear in them, fashionably dressed, and the calendars of saints' days in these books include scenes set in the countryside at appropriate times of the year. The famous *Très Riches Heures du Duc de Berry*, written shortly before 1416, shows richly dressed aristocrats going out hunting in August, while simply dressed peasants work in the fields or prepare to cool off in the river. Because they depict many figures, illuminated manuscripts are extremely important in helping us understand how different classes dressed and what clothes looked like from a variety of angles.

Individual portraits of royalty and the aristocracy began to emerge in the fourteenth century. In the fifteenth century, the wealthy middle classes also had their portraits painted. Everyone in these portraits tends to wear the most expensive clothing and jewelry that they can. Because the portraits are larger than figures in illuminated manuscripts, we get a better chance to study the details of fabric and construction, even the types of pins that held women's headdresses together. Portraits are often dated or datable.

Sculpted figures can help us understand how clothing looked in three dimensions. Sometimes a sculpture still has some of the paint in which it was originally covered, making the clothing on it even more "real." There are, however, problems in using sculpture to tell us about dress at a particular date, because we do not always know precisely when a sculpture was made. Even effigies on tombs are not always easy to date, because people could order them years before they died, or their families could order them years later.

We also can learn a lot from written sources. Chronicles and sermons by outraged churchmen tell us that people were interested in fashion and what the fashions were. Poets tell us of heroes and heroines and their clothes. Wills and inventories of possessions became quite common in the thirteenth

This 1888 painting by Ford Madox Brown is entitled *The Establishment of Flemish Weavers in Manchester in 1363.*

century. However, these sources give us relatively few details about how much it cost to buy fabric and make it into particular garments.

RULES AND REGULATIONS

There are many documents from the thirteenth century relating to the making of clothing. The guild regulations suggest that clothing designs had become more complex, and manufacture therefore had to be controlled more carefully. The wardrobe accounts of great households show a great variety of garments, not all of which can be identified today. These accounts can help us to understand how often new clothes were made, what they cost, the kinds of fabric used, and whether or not the time of year affected the choice of fabric and color. It has been calculated that in the fourteenth century it took about half a day to make a pair of hose, half a day to a day to make a hood, and three to six days to make a cloak, depending on whether or not it was lined.

Laws regulating dress are recorded from the mid-1100s onward. Sometimes states were trying to prevent too much money from being spent on clothes, or they were trying to stop people who were not of high enough social standing from wearing expensive fabrics and fashionable styles. In countries such as England and Scotland, which had to import silks from Italy, the laws sometimes stated that the aim was to prevent the country from becoming poor because money was going abroad to buy foreign goods.

In Italy, where the silks were made, the reasons could be different. Venice and Genoa relied on trade for their wealth. They felt that too much money was being spent on finery instead of being used in trade. A Florentine law of 1459 declared that, in a republic whose wealth came from trade, women were dressing less like the wives and daughters of merchants and private citizens, and more like the wives and daughters of princes and great lords.

The garments taken from the thirteenth-century royal tombs at Burgos in Spain include extremely rare surviving examples of complete outfits. A

This fourteenth century illustration by Giovannino de Grassi from the *Tacuinum Sanitatis*, a book mainly on health, depicts a tailor shop specializing in wool clothing.

A banquet scene shows people of the Netherlands feasting, and provides a view of the typical garb worn during the late middle ages.

doublet now in the Musée Historique des Tissus in Lyons, and associated with the Blessed Charles de Blois, who died in 1364, is of a very rare and costly fabric, Tartar cloth, imported from the Far East. The gold thread in it is almost pure gold. A few fourteenth-century garments have been removed from graves in Greenland, but we usually have to content ourselves with scraps of fabric and shoes excavated from medieval rubbish dumps.

Clothing was very costly by our standards, but sources show that people were slowly becoming wealthier and that fashionable dress was available to more people. Some people look back on the fashions of previous generations as a model of simplicity and virtue. If we really look at the evidence from the past, we would realize that they were considered extravagant in their own day.

CHAPTER TWO

THE ORIGINS OF FASHION

Medieval garb often consisted of several layers. The first layer (closest to the skin) for both men and women was an undershirt made of linen. Many men also wore linen underpants. Men and women alike wore woolen stockings on their legs. Women's stockings were usually knee-high. Over time, men's stockings grew longer and longer, while their upper layers grew shorter. At some point, many medieval men had entirely transitioned from stockings to tights. Depictions of medieval women often leave out the shoes, mainly because they were seldom seen, usually covered by long skirts. Only peasants and poor women wore skirts short enough for their feet to be seen. Men's shoes ranged from plain to very flamboyant (showy).

On top of their undershirts men could wear a jacket called a doublet, with or without an undertunic, which usually had full-length sleeves. Women also wore an undertunic. On top of that men and women wore an overtunic, which sometimes had sleeves and

This engraving shows a cross-section of the types of clothing worn by members of the French court during the 13th century.

sometimes didn't. The names of these tunics changed over the years, but the layers remained the same. For warmth many garments were fur-lined.

Out of doors, various cloaks might be worn. There were even cloaks to wear in the rain, but there is no evidence that they were truly waterproof. Most men wore some kind of head covering out of doors. Even indoors, women who were married were expected to cover their heads in veils or headdresses of some kind.

Throughout the Middle Ages and for centuries to come, all clothes were made from natural fibers: linen,

A FASHION BACKLASH

Around 1100 we see the first signs of the major alterations in appearance that provoked the fury of the Church when young men across Europe began wearing long tight-fitting garments with long trailing sleeves and shoes with turned-up toes, which made them walk in an affected way. They also began to grow their hair so long that they often looked like women. They combed their hair daily and they even had it artificially curled. On Easter Day, 1102, Henry I of England, in response to a sermon about longhaired men, allowed a bishop to cut his hair, and his courtiers followed his example.

Medieval society disapproved of people who strayed across the boundaries of their own social group, whether it was a peasant imitating a knight or, as seems to be the case here, men imitating women. In reality, however, these men, if they were not involved in warfare, did not need clothing or hairstyles that would allow them to be as physically active as their ancestors had been at the time of the Norman conquest of England in 1066. The upper classes, both men and women, from that time onward found many ways of dressing that indicated that they did not have to work.

A tailor in his shop examines the sleeves of a client. Measurements were always needed before the advent of mass production.

wool, and silk. Cotton was sometimes used, often as cotton-wool padding in doublets. There were also fabrics with mixed fibers. Clothes made from linen were the only ones washed regularly.

In the Early Middle Ages women wore loose-fitting garments. Eventually they began to wear tight clothing, with long sleeve ends, long plaits, and long veils. Female figures of the mid-1100s carved into Chartres Cathedral near Paris wear undertunics with very tight sleeves and skirts set in tiny pleats. Sometimes the tight bodices look as though they have been smocked, or pleated. This fabric is called chainse in poems from the twelfth century and would have been very expesive because of the tight, elaborate pleating. Smocking would certainly have given a degree of stretchiness to the clothing. Excavations in Scandinavia have revealed pieces of cloth from this time, set in narrow pleats and held in place with running stitches. Many poets refer to garments made of silk. The light silk known as cendal would have been ideal for fine pleating.

Poetry in France and Germany from about 1160 onward talks of women with very slender bodies encased in very tight clothing. Here the tightness of fit was achieved by lacing garments down the arms and sides, apparently so tightly as to cause pain. It seems that often the undershirt, and sometimes even the bare skin, was visible between the laces. Starting with Chrétien de Troyes's *Yvain,* of around 1170, poems suggest that it was usual to have a needle and thread handy so that sleeves could be sewn up tightly after garments were put on.

The artificiality of women's appearances may have led to a more general acceptance of makeup. A woman doctor who lived in the Italian city of Salerno around the year 1100 is said to have offered beauty hints that included how to get your cheeks the "correct" shade of pink (apply leeches if the cheeks are too red) and how to make hair blonde. According to *The Art of Love*, written by Andrew the Chaplain in France around 1185, a wise man would avoid a woman who used too much makeup, because a woman who relied on her makeup usually lacked gifts of personality.

Another part of fashionable dressing involved the use of fine furs, such as sable, ermine, and gray squirrel, known as miniver. In 1188, knights intending to go on crusade were forbidden to wear miniver or sable furs, or scarlet cloth. King John of England, who reigned from 1199 to 1216, is known to have spent two pounds on a single sable skin. It would take a carpenter of the time about 120 days of work to save that amount! For his two pounds, the king could also have bought about six yards of scarlet.

Color in dress was important for those who could afford it. Between 1158 and 1188, Henry II of England bought ruby scarlets (dyed with kermes), black scarlets, and perse (blue) scarlets. The scarlets cost up to three times as much as *say* (another woolen fabric), even when the say had been dyed in kermes. Other says were green or gray, and other fabrics were violet, dark gray, and brown. An Italian inventory of 1176 includes clothes dyed blue with indigo. The colors of dress at this time were often bright and recalled the vivid colors of contemporary stained glass windows.

REGULATING WARDROBES

Extremely tight clothing disappeared around 1200, to be replaced by looser clothing that was fitted only at the wrists. However, these looser styles disappeared within a generation in a new quest for tightly fitting clothing. Buttons were used at the neck, and toward the end of the century they were used on the lower arms to fasten clothing and make it neater in those areas. A typical aristocratic gesture of the thirteenth century involved hooking the thumb of one hand into the cord that held the cloak together at the neck, as though the weight was in danger of pulling the cloak backward and choking its wearer. Together, the cloak, overtunic, and undertunic formed a suit, or robe. Clothing was clearly becoming more complex, and we should not be surprised that attempts to control it in earnest began at this time.

In 1204, the soldiers of the Fourth Crusade sacked the city of Constantinople. The massive amount of booty they captured included silks and cloaks of squirrel fur and ermine. This seems to have led to an increase in the desire to own such luxuries in western Europe. The effects could be seen within a generation.

Figured silks were still a rarity, but they were worn in great numbers for the coronation of Louis VIII of France in 1223. In 1229, Louis IX of France, later known as St. Louis, tried to limit the extravagance of aristocratic clothing. Jean Sire de Joinville's *Life of St. Louis* tells us of an occasion when, as a young man, he was criticized by a fellow courtier for being more richly dressed than the king. The king, however, argued that it was a nobleman's duty to dress well. Joinville tells us that usually Louis wore a cloak of black cendal, but for special occasions he might put on a cloak of vermilion samite, lined with ermine, which was much more in keeping with his status. Joinville also says that after Louis returned from a Crusade in 1254, he refused to wear ermine or squirrel fur,

This section of an illuminated manuscript shows the coronation of French monarch Louis VIII and his bride, Blanche of Castille.

preferring much cheaper lambskin or hare skin. He also refused to wear scarlet.

SUBVERTING CLASS

In Germany in 1244, it was decreed that peasants should have short-cropped hair and gray, simple clothing. The German satirical poem *Helmbrecht* deals with a peasant who apes his social superiors by having shoulder-length hair, on which he wears a cap decorated with battle scenes. He also uses silver buttons. He really is dressing beyond his class, as silver buttons were bought for the children of King Edward I of England in the 1270s, and decorated caps have been found in royal tombs in Spain. Helmbrecht becomes the leader of a group of bandits who steal from the peasants. The peasants finally kill him. The poem indicates that the crossing of social boundaries cannot go unpunished.

A number of women's fashions also became the objects of legal attention—for example, the trains on their clothes and their crownlike headdresses. Women seem to have been quite clever at getting around the laws. A local chronicle tells us that in 1278 the Church ordered all the female inhabitants of Parma to wear veils, in the interests of modesty. This upset the women at first, but they found a way around it. They made fine veils, interwoven with gold, which made them look even more attractive and made men look at them even more!

Those who made such clothes were also subject to controls, through the craft guilds. Although in Florence the tailors were not considered important enough to have their own guild, in 1219 the tailors in Venice had their own rules governing the making of garments. The *Livre des Métiers* (*Book of Crafts*), compiled around 1260 in Paris, mentions makers of silk hairnets and those who worked with silk cloth and velvet (velvet first appeared around this time). The tailor of robes was separated from the tailor of furred robes. In many cities tailors of robes were separate from makers of doublets. Because doublets were quilted, doubletmakers could belong to the guild of quiltmakers. Hosemakers often belonged to yet another guild.

In 1281, Venetian capmakers were ordered not to sell old caps as new ones, nor Tuscan ones as English ones. In 1292, the embroiderers of Paris banned working in poor light. In 1323, to prevent customers from being cheated, the tailors of robes in Paris were ordered to tack a sample of all the inner linings on to garment collars.

Merchants and craftsmen, however, clearly did cheat their customers. People everywhere complained that cloth merchants used a short measuring stick when they were selling cloth and a long stick when they were buying it. There were complaints that they sold their goods in dark corners so that customers could not see the quality of the goods, and that they tried to sell inferior quality cloth as better quality cloth.

Agnes Sorel, the mistress of King Charles VII of France, is shown in this colored engraving dressed for court, with the very long tail of her headdress trailing behind her

Some items of clothing could be bought ready-made, but making it was not encouraged, perhaps because of the scope for cheating. In Montauban in France in the early fourteenth century, the Bonis brothers sold both cloth and ready-made underwear. They also sold doublets. In 1443 in Bourges in France, the hosemakers and cloth merchants were allowed to make hose for sale, but they were not to use old fabric. The medieval French farce *Maistre Pathelin* is about a lawyer trying to get hold of cloth to be made into clothes for himself and his wife, by cheating a cloth merchant.

CHAPTER THREE

NEW, OUTRAGEOUS, AND OUTLANDISH

In every era, it seems that young people are chastised for their fashion choices, especially by their elders. In western Europe around 1340 CE, there was constant criticism of new fashions among youth. Some blamed it on foreign influences. One monarch, King Robert of Naples had declared in 1335 that young men's clothing had become exaggerated, even ridiculous. One complaint was that their top garments barely reached beneath their buttocks. Another was the ever increasing tightness of their clothes.

A resident of Florence, Giovanni Villani, told of the rule of Frenchman Walter de Brienne from 1342 to 1343 CE, during which knights favored a guarnacca. This was an Italian tunic that was tight enough that they needed assistance to don it. English monk, theologian, and philosopher John of Reading, said that when the Queen of England's followers from the Low Countries (the Netherlands and Belgium) came to the royal court around 1327, they had sparked a fashion craze among the native English. By 1344, gone were the long, modest, and full fashions of yesteryear, replaced with short, tight, impractical, and often tightly laced clothing. The new fashion was overtunics with buttoned sleeves and tippets—long tails hanging from the sleeves at the wearer's elbows—along with very long hoods. Critics of these new fashions felt the young people were filled with too much pride and vanity, and that they ended up absurd in appearance.

When the French were defeated by the English at the Battle of Crécy in 1346, the French writer of the *Grandes Chroniques de France* said that the

The fashion favored by some English men during the early reign of Edward III in the mid-fourteenth century was notable for the bands of material attached to sleeves that hung down to the knees.

French had lost because of their pride. And their pride stemmed from their clothing, which was so tight that men had to be helped to dress and undress. When they were being undressed it looked as though they were being skinned. The tails on their hoods and sleeves were so long that they looked like entertainers. In fact, tailors were now, for the first time ever, able to produce clothing that fit properly, and they seem to have taken their pride in their abilities just a bit too far, producing wildly impractical clothing that some later writers have seen as the start of true fashion.

Yet another flourish in men's costumes is displayed here on a man during the reign of Richard II (1377–1399). He wears a houppelande, a full-bodied garment with big, flared sleeves. Women also wore them.

FINDING FAULT

One might have expected that when men decided to wear longer, looser, more flowing garments, the complaints would come to an end. Not at all. Around 1360, such garments came into fashion, and in English they were called gouns, pronounced "goons," a term of mockery. In France such a garment was called a houppelande; in Italy it was called a pellanda. Both men and women wore them, though men could wear houppelandes that stopped at the buttocks. Women's houppelandes, as with all their clothing, had to reach the floor. The garment was also criticized because it made men look like women from behind. If men responded to criticism of the houppelande by wearing another new fashion, a short doublet-like garment called a paltock, they were also likely to be criticized. This was too short, according to the critics. One critic objected to the *mi-parti* (multi-colored) hose that men tied to the paltock. These hose were called in English by various names, all of which meant "worthless fellows."

Once again, John of Reading's chronicle blamed foreign influence for the fashions worn in 1365. Men were wearing tiny hoods, buttoned extremely tight under the chin. However, it was men's shoes that continued to annoy the authorities, because the toes grew ever longer. A new type of long-toed shoe, called a cracow in England and a poulaine in France, seems to have become fashionable in 1362. In that year, these shoes were denounced as being more like the nails of demons than ornaments for people. In 1365, a Church meeting at Angers in France tried to ban them. In 1366, the king of France banned their use in Paris, and he also banned the making of them.

A young man displays many of the elaborate touches common to those who wished to look elegant in the later middle ages.

A poem written in England in 1388 complained that men were unable to kneel to pray because their long toes got in the way, and also because they were afraid that the tight laces holding their doublets to their hose might split. In the same year a chronicler in the Italian city of Piacenza noted how short and tight the doublets of young men were, and that the toes of their shoes were so long that it was necessary to stuff them with horse hair to stop them from bending.

During the siege of Nicopolis in 1396, the French knights found that they had to cut off the toes of their shoes (over two feet long, according to the *Chronicle of the Monk of Saint-Denis*) if they wanted to walk easily in battle. The same commentator noted that they also wore garments with sleeves of unreasonable length (as did young men around 1100). While some long-toed French knights were at Nicopolis, other fashionable men at home in France were being criticized by the poet Eustache Deschamps for the way those long toes made them walk sideways like crabs. A manuscript of 1395–1396 in the British Library shows Richard II of England with his courtiers. Two of the goun-wearing courtiers have toes that are so long that the artist has painted them coming out beyond the edge of the picture!

Men gave out signals by covering or uncovering their heads. When the pope visited the staunchly republican city of Genoa in 1272, the Genoese kept their heads covered because they thought that to uncover their heads was a sign of servility to the pope. When the humanist scholar and republican politician Palla Strozzi was exiled from Florence in 1434 for opposing Medici rule and went to Padua, he was amazed to find that men of all ranks in that city uncovered their heads to him, so greatly did they respect him. This was certainly not the custom in republican Florence, where all men, at least of the governing class, were considered equal. From the Low Countries in the fifteenth century, we find pictures where only Philip the Good, duke of Burgundy, keeps his head covered, even indoors, among his courtiers. The French king Charles VIII charmed the ladies of the ducal court of Milan when he met them in 1494, as he insisted on taking off his hat to greet them. To him ladies, even of much lower rank, were entitled to this courtesy by virtue of their sex.

In Florence in 1462, there was great excitement at the return from France of the ambassadors sent to congratulate Louis XI on becoming king. The ambassadors had left Florence in Florentine style clothing, provided at the city's expense. One of the ambassadors had persuaded the others to change into French-style clothing when they reached southern France. It was in this French clothing that they appeared before

FASHIONABLE FIGHTING WORDS

Besides telling the world that you were rich and fashionable (or neither), medieval clothing could tell the world about your politics, your feelings, and your status within a group. In the early fifteenth century, France saw two of its royal dukes competing to govern the country because the king suffered from attacks of madness. The dukes used clothing to send messages to each other. The duke of Orléans decorated his clothing with an embroidered image of a wooden club and the words "I challenge you" in French. The duke of Burgundy, in reply, decorated his clothing with the words "I accept the challenge" in Flemish, with miniature carpenters' planes all over the surface to show that he would cut away at the Orléans club. In 1413, the members of the city council of Paris ordered clothing for themselves to show that they supported the duke of Orléans. They used one of his livery colors, violet, and had another of his mottos, *Le droit chemin*, "the straight road," embroidered on this violet clothing.

Many years later, in 1462, the duke of Burgundy's grandson, Philip the Good, fell out with his son Charles. Philip attended a wedding wearing his usual black clothing, with the addition of a cap covered in teardrops. People who saw this very public display understood it to mean that his son,

who should have been the source of his joy, had become the source of his sorrows. In 1473, when he went to meet Emperor Frederick III, Charles dressed his courtiers in an intricate arrangement of colors and fabrics. A man wearing a crimson velvet doublet and black hose was more important than a man wearing a crimson satin doublet and black hose because velvet was more expensive than satin. But he was less important than a man wearing a black satin doublet and a crimson velvet gown, because the crimson velvet gown required more fabric than the crimson velvet doublet.

Louis XI. Louis seems to have been delighted by this gesture, which suggested sympathy with France. They were still wearing their French clothes when they returned to Florence, and everyone rushed out into the streets to stare at them as they passed by. French clothes were thought to be unstylish and indecently short. The ambassadors, in abandoning the clothing styles of their homeland, must have seemed like traitors, as well as appearing rather badly dressed.

Brides going to marry abroad were expected to change into the fashions of their new country as soon as possible, to show their new loyalties. There used to be wall paintings near Milan that showed the arrival of Bona of Savoy from France as the bride of the duke of Milan in 1469. Among those paintings was a scene

A young couple displays fashion typical of the middle of the fifteenth century.

of Bona changing from French-style clothing into Milanese-style clothing. We know from written records that the duke even hired a servant who could help her arrange her hair and headdress in the Milanese fashion.

Mourning clothing told everyone instantly that you had lost a relative or a friend. Mourning was a frequent element in people's lives, and it had its own colors, some of them rather surprising to us. Not all mourning clothes were black. When the kings of France died, their widows would wear white and their heirs could wear purple. At the funeral of a king of France, the chief judges wore their scarlet judges' robes because the king's justice was still alive.

In 1465, the queen of Naples died just when she was expected to welcome her new daughter-in-law, Ippolita Maria Sforza. The Neapolitan princess, Leonora of Aragon, had to perform the ceremony of welcome instead of her dead mother. Perhaps as a compromise between joy and sorrow, Leonora wore a dress of gold cloth with a background of morello, a reddish-purple, under a morello overgarment. In Ferrara in the late 1460s, we find Leonora's brother-in-law, Borso, the

This fresco by Benozzo Gozzoli from 1459, *The Cavalcade of the Magi*, shows the annual post-Christmas street parade common in Spain, including a great diversity of men's head gear.

marquis of Ferrara, wearing morello as mourning for two friends. Leonora herself, in later life, often wore black, but she was not in mourning.

When Borso died in 1471, his body was dressed in a crimson and cloth of gold cloak, with a hood and collar of miniver. Even though he had asked to be buried naked, as a final rejection of the splendor with which he had lived, he was buried in rose-colored scarlet cloth. Borso had been a prince who had lived and dressed splendidly, as it was a prince's duty to do, and he could not be allowed to appear before his people for the last time in anything but clothes befitting his rank. Clothing thus told those who were "in the know" many different things.

CHAPTER FOUR

ROYAL RAIMENT AND LAVISH ATTIRE

As clothing itself became more elaborate, so did the rituals and procedures for getting dressed, along with the manufacturing of the highly desired and thus expensive fabrics. A high-ranking member of the Florentine elite, Alessandra Macinghi negli Strozzi, became famous for her letters detailing her efforts to maintain her family's economic station. Among many other rich details of the period, the letters reveal that her daughter Caterina had been engaged to a young silk merchant in 1447, Marco Parenti. His own accounts plus her mother's show that he decided to have the finest fabric provided to his fiancée in his own shop.

This turned out to be a crimson figured velvet transformed into a cotta, an undertunic, requiring eleven yards of the material. Embroidered with pearls and trimmed at the hem with green and gold fringe, it was topped off by a giornea, an open-sided sleeveless garment requiring fifteen yards of cloth, trimmed with a lettice, a white fur. Both pieces were lined in, red and the bride also had a garland of feathers and pearls. To imagine the opulence of this outfit, note that Caterina's dowry (which was supposed to provide enough money to live on for many years) was about 1,000 florins (the currency of Florence at the time), while her wedding garments totaled more than 400 florins. The family may have regretted this extravagance later, because Marco Parenti later sold many of his wife's clothes.

This miniature from an Italian manuscript of the fourteenth century shows a wedding attended by members of the nobility.

In 1469, Alessandra's daughter-in-law Fiametta tried to get out of going to the wedding of the decade, that of Lorenzo de Medici to Clarice Orsini, because she feared the cost of the clothes that she would have to buy. Everyone was busy having garments made of brocade, and the festivities would last nearly three weeks. In this time the guests would have to change their outfits several times. In the end she did go, and she must have been among the crowd whose appearance contributed to the sour observation made by Marco Parenti's son, Piero, that the lavishness of this wedding was more appropriate to a princely court.

We can glimpse what a truly princely wedding was like from the trousseau created four years before, when Ippolita Maria Sforza, daughter of the duke of Milan, married the heir to the kingdom of Naples. Ippolita's dowry was worth 200,000 florins. About 66,000 of these florins were in the form of her clothes and jewels. Everything was listed, with its value. Two of her gowns were so valuable that they weren't listed among her clothes, but among her jewels. These two gowns were of crimson silk. The more valuable one had very wide sleeves "like wings," which were lined with a green damask brocaded in gold. The bodice was embroidered with almost 9,000 pearls and with gold and silver thread that weighed 70 ounces.

Following the practices that he had seen at the Burgundian court, King Edward IV of England began reorganizing his own household staff in 1478. He had two catagories—the wardrobe of robes and the wardrobe of beds. Members of the wardrobes staff

DRESSING AN ARISTOCRAT

The actual dressing of an aristocrat was a serious matter. In 1450, when Ippolita's brother, Galeazzo Maria, was six years old, their father became duke of Milan. There was an official discussion about giving the child his own courtiers, including people whose job it would be to dress him. His senior tutor felt that it would take three people to dress him, but other advisers thought it would take more. There was the servant who brought in his underclothes every day. Then two people would be needed to hold him while he was dressed. One servant held his shoes. Another servant held his stockings. Another was needed to hold his vestito, or gown, and another servant buttoned him up. The more important you were, the more people you had doing things for you, but it also looks as though Galeazzo Maria was likely to wriggle and be difficult to dress! There used to be a wall painting that showed him getting dressed when he was a grown man and the duke of Milan, and, we hope, better behaved.

had to wash, clean, and mend the king's clothes and see that his robes, doublets, shirts, and sheets were kept perfumed with herbs all year round. Servants called Esquires of the Body had to dress and undress the king, and had to watch over him day and night.

The English king employed a figure called a chamberlain, whose duties, like those of the Esquires of the Body, included the complete dressing of the king. First of all, the chamberlain had to make sure that the king's clothes were clean and his hose well brushed. Then he was to put a linen sheet over the king's chair beside the fire and put down cushions for the king's feet. When the king was at the fireside, the chamberlain helped him into his underwear, his doublet, and then his stomacher, a piece of cloth worn on the chest for extra warmth. Then the chamberlain put on the king's hose and shoes and laced or buckled them. He then pulled the hose up the king's legs until they could be tied to the doublet at the waist. Then the doublet had to be carefully laced closed. Only after all this was done would the chamberlain kneel before the king and ask what else he wished to wear that day.

ISABELLA AND BEATRICA D'ESTE

Italy seems to have been far more active in trying to control fashion, especially women's fashions, than the northern European states. In spite of this, it is from Italy at the end of the fifteenth century that we get very clear ideas of the importance of clothing, in the lives of women in particular. We also get a glimpse of how new fashions were created. This information can be found in letters written about the sisters Isabella and Beatrice d'Este, and in letters they wrote to each other in the 1490s after their marriages took them to

Bianca Maria Sforza was the empress of the Holy Roman Empire. Her jeweled headdress was valued around 600 ducats, a small fortune then.

different cities. Isabella and Beatrice were two prominent noble ladies of the late fifteenth century. Isabella married Francesco Gonzaga, the marquis of Mantua, and Beatrice married Lodovico Sforza of Milan.

The two sisters loved clothes, and Isabella developed the reputation of being the best-dressed woman in Italy. Early in her married life in Milan, Beatrice and her cousin decided to go shopping in the city, disguised as middle-class women. It began to rain and the two girls put cloths over their heads to protect themselves. Apparently this was not common in Milan, and some local women began shouting insults at them. Beatrice returned home furious. We hear no more about attempts to dress outside her social class.

In 1492, a cousin suggested that a pattern of chains could be worked into Isabella's clothing. A year later, when Beatrice didn't feel like "inventing" anything new, she wrote to ask Isabella if she had used the chain design yet. Would she allow Beatrice to use it, if she hadn't used it herself, for a dress to wear to a family wedding? When Beatrice heard of a new headdress worn by the queen of France, her husband wrote to his contact at the French court, asking for details and a drawing of it, because Beatrice wanted one like it. Beatrice, married to the most powerful man in Milan, once sat up all night to finish making clothing for a court festivity!

In 1493, two years after she was married, Beatrice took her mother, Leonora of Aragon, to see a room in which she kept only some of the garments she had acquired since her marriage. In this room alone there were over eighty gowns and cloaks. Leonora remarked rather sharply that the room looked more like the sacristy of a church, where the rich vestments used by priests would be stored. Despite this jibe, Beatrice would often turn to her mother for advice. Her mother's embroiderer had designed a pattern of flowers to be worked into one of Beatrice's dresses, and her own embroiderer had said that the pattern would have to be altered to be smaller on the bodice than on the skirt. What did her mother think? Professionals such as this embroiderer probably had vital

In this image, the chamberlain assists a king in the left panel with his shoes, while a duke gives the king spurs in the right.

parts to play in the creation of new styles, because they would know what could and what couldn't be made.

When their mother died in 1493, the young women were heartbroken, but they were still anxious to know what each other's mourning attire looked like. Beatrice herself died at the age of only twenty-two, soon after childbirth, in 1497. There is a carving of her on a tomb in Pavia near Milan, made soon after her death. She is shown wearing a dress that is said to be one she wore to celebrate the birth of her first son in 1493. Isabella was told that it consisted of horizontal bands of cloth of gold and crimson velvet. Over the crimson velvet lay a network of silver threads, which stopped when they reached the gold cloth. They then hung like fringing over the gold cloth.

"INVENTOR OF NEW CLOTHES"

Beatrice's husband seems to have been proud of her and her interest in fashion. A contemporary who did not like her at all dismissed her as an empty-headed "inventor of new clothes." But she was young, she had access to a great deal of money, and she had a husband who was happy to let her spend it. She was simply expressing, in an unusually determined way, what the Middle Ages felt about dress.

Isabella had less money to spend than Beatrice and therefore she was more selective and less extravagant. She used family contacts to buy the most exquisite fabrics wherever they went. If other people had some-

This detail of an altarpiece from the 15th century shows Beatrice d'Este kneeling as a donor to the church. The image is notable because she is dressed in fashionable clothing, and not more pious and somber garb.

thing, she said, she didn't want it. By 1506, Isabella's reputation as the judge of all matters of taste in dress was secure. Women would ask her to supervise the making of their clothes and to let them wear fashions that she had invented. The queen of Poland called her "the source and origin of all the beautiful fashions in Italy." Even the king of France asked Isabella to dress a doll as she herself dressed, so that he could have some outfits like Isabella's made for French ladies.

Isabella knew that as a woman she would have little real power in a man's world of politics. By constantly reminding everyone how interested she was in art, she gained the respect of many of the leading scholars of the day, who were almost all men. By making a work of art of herself and her clothes, she gained the respect of women and of many men; even kings wanted to know how she dressed. Isabella and Beatrice typified the attitude of many noble ladies during the Middle Ages, who believed that clothing was a form of display used to separate oneself from those of lesser stature, and even within one's own class to display one's superiority and uniqueness. The goals of fashion have not changed much in 500 years.

GLOSSARY

brocade A category of rich and decorative woven fabrics, usually silk, often with intricate patterns.

cendal A lightweight silk, often used to make banners and decorations and to line clothes.

chainse A type of woman's dress, mentioned in poems of the twelfth century.

churching A ceremony marking a woman's first attendance at church after childbirth.

cotta An Italian term for the undertunic that was in use from the thirteenth century.

cotton-wool A product of the cotton plant, grown in India in the Middle Ages.

crimson A very expensive dye made from the kermes insect.

damask A patterned silk, almost always made in one color.

doublet A short underjacket, related to the quilted jackets used under armor.

dowry A sum of money given by a bride's parents to her husband.

embroidery The decoration of a fabric by colored threads introduced by a needle.

ermine The white winter coat of a member of the weasel family.

figured silk The general term for any silk on which there is a pattern.

finish Treatments applied to woolen cloths to improve their appearance.

florin The monetary currency of Florence from 1252

CE to 1533 CE.

furrier A craftsman who made up furs into sheetlike panels and sold them.

fustian A mixed-fiber fabric, often made in Germany.

giornea An Italian term for an open-sided, sleeveless garment worn first by soldiers and then by fashionable men and women.

goun/gown An English term for a full-length garment worn by men and women. By 1400 CE, it had developed very wide sleeves that looked like triangles from the side.

guarnacca An association of craftsmen operating under a set of rules, who also helped mentor apprentices to their craft.

illuminated manuscript A handwritten text with pictures painted on the pages.

indigo An expensive plant-based blue dye.

kermes The most expensive medieval dye, producing strong reds, and derived from the dried bodies of insects.

lettice A white fur, sometimes used in place of ermine.

linen A fabric produced from the stems of the flax plant.

miniver A Siberian squirrel fur, very fashionable until the early fifteenth century.

paltock One of a number of short jacketlike garments worn by men in the later fourteenth century.

robe A French term for a suit of clothes in the thirteenth and fourteenth centuries. After about 1430, it came to mean a sleeved outer garment.

sable The fur of a member of the marten family. The most prized sables were black.

samite A rich medieval silk fabric interwoven with gold or silver.

scarlet The most expensive woolen cloth, as expensive as some silks.

smocking A technique by which the edges of fine pleats in cloth are stitched together at intervals, often in fancy patterns.

tippets Long tails hanging from the backs of hoods and from the elbows of sleeves in the fourteenth century.

vermillion A bright red fabric.

vestito An Italian term for a garment, usually the equivalent of a northern European gown in the fifteenth century.

wardrobe account A list of purchased fabrics, with their costs and what they were made into, kept by those handling the clothing of great lords and rulers.

Canadian Society of Medievalists
c/o Roisin Cossar
Department of History
University of Manitoba
454 Fletcher Argue Building
Winnipeg, MB R3T 5V5
Website: http://www.canadianmedievalists.ca
The Canadian Society of Medievalists is an academic organization dedicated to promoting excellence in research for all aspects of medieval studies.

Columbia University Medieval Colloquium
602 Philosophy Hall
Columbia University
New York, NY 10027
Website: http://blogs.cuit.columbia.edu/medguild
The Medieval Colloquium (formerly the Medieval Guild) of Columbia University is a graduate student organization for medievalists whose mission is to help students develop professionally in their research about this historical period.

International Center of Medieval Art (ICMA)
The Cloisters, Fort Tryon Park
99 Margaret Corbin Drive
New York, NY 10040
(212) 928-1146
Website: http://www.medievalart.org
The International Center of Medieval Art promotes and

supports the study, understanding, and preservation of the visual and material cultures of medieval Europe, including the Mediterranean region and the Slavic world.

Medieval Academy of America
17 Dunster Street, Suite 202
Cambridge, MA 02138
(617) 491-1622
Website: http://www.medievalacademy.org
The Medieval Academy of America is the largest organization in the United States promoting excellence in medieval studies, including fostering research, publication, and teaching in medieval art archaeology, history, law, literature, music, philosophy, religion, science, social and economic institutions.

Rocky Mountain Medieval and Renaissance Association
c/o Jennifer McNabb
Department of History
Western Illinois University
438 Morgan Hall
1 University Circle
Macomb, IL 61455
E-mail: Jl-mcnabb@wiu.edu
Website: http://www.rmmra.org
The Rocky Mountain Medieval & Renaissance Association is a nonprofit, academic organization dedicated to the advancement of learning in the fields of Medieval and Renaissance studies.

Society for Creative Anachronism (SCA)
P.O. Box 360789
Milpitas, CA 95036
(408) 263-9305
Website: http://www.sca.org
The Society for Creative Anachronism is an international organization dedicated to researching and recreating the arts and skills of pre-seventeenth century Europe.

WEBSITES

Because of the changing number of internet links, Rosen Publishing has developed an online list of websites related to the subject of this book. This site is updated regularly. Please use this link to access this list:

http://www.rosenlinks.com/LMID/cloth

FOR FURTHER READING

Allen, Nicole, and Gregory Mele. *The Book of Historic Fashion: A Newcomer's Guide to Medieval Clothing 1300 – 1450*. Wheaton, IL: Freelance Academy Press, 2014.

Basing, Patricia. *Trades and Crafts in Medieval Manuscripts*. London, United Kingdom: The British Library, 1990.

Evans, Joan. *Dress in Mediaeval France*. Oxford, United Kingdom: Clarendon Press, 1952.

Harris, Jennifer, ed. *5000 Years of Textiles*. London, United Kingdom: British Museum Press, 1993.

Koslin, D., and Janet Snyder (eds.). *Encountering Medieval Textiles and Dress: Objects, Texts, Images* (The New Middle Ages). New York, NY: Palgrave Macmillan, 2009.

Netherton, Robin and Gale R. Owen-Crocker (eds.). *Medieval Clothing and Textiles 11*. Suffolk, United Kingdom: Boydell Press, 2015.

Piponnier, Françoise, and Perrine Mane. *Dress in the Middle Ages*. New Haven, CT: Yale University Press, 1997.

Scott, Margaret. *Fashion in the Middle Ages*. Malibu, CA: J. Paul Getty Museum, 2011.

Staniland, Kay. *Medieval Craftsmen: Embroiderers*. London, United Kingdom: British Museum Press, 1991.

Steele, Philip. *The Medieval World: Volume 1* (History of Costume and Fashion). New York, NY: Facts on File, 2005.

BIBLIOGRAPHY

Andreas Capellanus. *The Art of Courtly Love*. New York, NY: W. W. Norton and Company, 1941.

Birdsall, Jean, translator, and Richard A Newhall, ed. *The Chronicle of Jean de Venette*. New York, NY: Columbia University Press, 1953.

Brucker, Gene. *Florence: The Golden Age, 1138–1737*. Berkeley, CA: University of California Press, 1998.

Campbell, Lorne. *Renaissance Portraits: European Portrait-Painting in the 14th, 15th and 16th Centuries*. New Haven, CT: Yale University Press, 1990.

Cartwright, Julia (Mrs. Henry Ady). *Isabella d'Este, Marchioness of Mantua 1474–1539: A Study of the Renaissance*. London, United Kingdom: J. Murray, 1904.

Cartwright, Julia (Mrs. Henry Ady). *Beatrice d'Este, Duchess of Milan, 1475–1497: A Study of the Renaissance*. London, United Kingdom: J. M. Dent and Co., 1905.

Dyer, Christopher. *Standards of Living in the Later Middle Ages: Social Change in England c.1200–1520*. Cambridge, United Kingdom: Cambridge University Press, 1989.

Eco, Umberto. *Art and Beauty in the Middle Ages*. New Haven, CT: Yale University Press, 1986.

Goddard, Eunice. *Women's Costume in French Texts of the Eleventh and Twelfth Centuries*. Johns Hopkins Studies in Romance Literatures and Languages. Baltimore, MD: The Johns Hopkins Press, 1927.

Goetz, Hans-Werner. *Life in the Middle Ages from the Seventh to the Thirteenth Century*. Translated by Albert Wimmer, edited by Steven Rowan. Notre Dame, IN: University of Notre Dame Press, 1993.

Herald, Jacqueline. *The History of Dress Series: Renaissance Dress in Italy 1400–1500*. London: Bell and Hyman and Humanities Press, 1981.

Kovesi Killerby, Catherine. *Sumptuary Law in Italy 1200–1500*. Oxford, United Kingdom: Clarendon Press, 2002.

Levi Pisetzky, Rosita. *Storia del Costume in Italia*. Vols 1–2. Milan, Italy: Istituto Editoriale Italiano, 1964.

Longnon, Jean, Raymond Cazelles, and Millard Meiss. *Les Très Riches Heures du Duc de Berry, Musée Condé, Chantilly*. London: Thames and Hudson, 1969.

Lubkin, Gregory. *A Renaissance Court: Milan under Galeazzo Maria Sforza*. Berkeley, CA: University of California Press, 1994.

Munro, John H. "The Medieval Scarlet and the Economics of Sartorial Splendour" in N. B. Harte and K. G. Ponting (eds), *Cloth and Clothing in Medieval Europe: Essays in Memory of Professor E. M. Carus-Wilson*. London, United Kingdom: Heinemann Educational Books, 1983, pp. 13–70.

Newton, Stella Mary. *Fashion in the Age of the Black Prince: A Study of the Years 1340–1365*. Totowa, NJ: Rowman and Littlefield, 1980.

Origo, Iris. *The Merchant of Prato: Francesco di Marco Dantini*. London, United Kingdom: Jonathan Cape and Penguin Books, 1957.

Phillips, Mark. *The Memoir of Marco Parenti: A Life in Renaissance Florence*. London, United Kingdom: Heinemann, 1989.

Ribeiro, Aileen. *Dress and Morality*. London, United Kingdom: Batsford, 1986.

Scott, Margaret. *The History of Dress Series: Late Gothic Europe, 1400–1500*. London: Mills and Boon, 1980.

Scott, Margaret. *A Visual History of Costume: The Fourteenth and Fifteenth Centuries*. London, United Kingdom: Batsford, 1986.

Vaughan, Richard. *Charles the Bold, the Last Valois Duke of Burgundy*. London, United Kingdom: Longman, 1973.

Vespasiano da Bisticci, Fiorentino. *The Vespasiano Memoirs: Lives of Illustrious Men of the XVth Century*. Translated by William George and Emily Waters. Introduction by Myron P. Gilmore. Toronto, ON, Canada: University of Toronto Press, 1997.

Welch, Evelyn Samuels. "Galeazzo Maria Sforza and the Castello of Pavia, 1469." *The Art Bulletin*, Vol. LXXXI, 1989, pp. 352–375

Welch, Evelyn S. *Art and Authority in Renaissance Milan*. New Haven, CT: Yale University Press, 1995.

INDEX

J

K

L

M

R

S

T

V

W

ABOUT THE AUTHORS

Margaux Baum is a writer and editor from Queens, New York.

Margaret Scott studied classics at Glasgow University and the history of dress at the Courtauld Institute of Art, London University. Dr. Scott is head of the History of Dress section at the Courtauld, and is an internationally recognized expert on medieval and Renaissance dress.

PHOTO CREDITS

Cover (silhouetted figures), pp. 20, 34 Private Collection/Bridgeman Images; cover (background) Tomasz Bidermann/Shutterstock.com; p. 3 Heather McCallum/Moment/Getty Images; pp. 4–5 (background) leoks/Shutterstock.com; p. 5 Print Collector/Hulton Fine Art Collection/Getty Images; pp. 7, 19, 30, 41 Bildagentur Zoonar GmbH/Shutterstock.com; p. 8 DEA/A. Villani/De Agostini Picture Library/Getty Images; p. 10 Bibliotheque Municipale, Dijon, France/Bridgeman Images; p. 15 Manchester Art Gallery, UK/Bridgeman Images; p. 17 DEA/G. Nimatallah/De Agostini Picture Library/Getty Images; p. 18 Musee Conde, Chantilly, France/Bridgeman Images; pp. 22, 25 Photo 12/Universal Images Group/Getty Images; p. 28 Private Collection/© Look and Learn/Bridgeman Images; p. 31 Print Collector/Hulton Archive/Getty Images; p. 32 Culture Club/ Hulton Archive/Getty Images; p. 38 Hulton Archive/Getty Images; p. 39 Palazzo Medici Riccardi, Florence/De Agostini Picture Library/G. Nimatallah/Bridgeman Images; p. 42 DEA/A. Dagli Orti/De Agostini Picture Library/Getty Images; p. 46 GraphicaArtis/Archive Photos/Getty Images; p. 48 Photo © Tallandier/Bridgeman Images; p. 50 DEA Picture Library/Getty Images; cover and interior pages flourishes and borders wenani/Shutterstock.com; interior pages fleur-de-lis riedjal/ Shutterstock.com; interior pages textures murengstockphoto/Shutterstock.com, LeksusTuss/ Shutterstock.com; back cover (background) © iStockphoto.com/MagMos; back cover (silhouette) Dikas Studio/Shutterstock.com.

Designer: Michael Moy; Editor: Philip Wolny; Photo Researcher: Philip Wolny